HIGH-PERFORM
CARS

Coloring Book Volume 1

By: CHANTIM IN

MW00769299

Also lookout for
"Trucks & SUVs"
Coming soon...

Acknowledgments

Special thanks to:
ADV.1 wheel industry Jordan Swerdloff / Mike Burroughs / and the whole ADV.1 team for providing the contents needed to make this coloring book come to life. Adv1wheels.com

Special dedication:
I would like to make this coloring book a dedication to my wife Kama Keo. Thank you so much Kama for standing by me and taking every step with me through this journey in life. I am truly blessed and grateful for all that you have done for us, you have worked so hard and sacrificed so much to get us to where we are right now. The love that comes from your heart is immeasurable...and as a registered nurse, I know that you are an Angel of Life by noticing that your patients appreciates you considerably as well from the gifts of gratitude you are always coming home with. To my sweet "Pumpkin", I truly appreciate you. Mmmmhh!!!

Last but not least, thank you Life for this present experience and for all the lessens that have brought me here. I am now awaken to the beauty of all things and all life forms that surrounds me.

Introduction

Growing up, I had always been into drawing and coloring. I can recall just about all of the times that I drew cars, trucks, motorcycles, and even planes on the back of my classrooms' assignments. Some of my teachers were kind enough to make uplifting comments about it and some even threaten me to go see the principle's office. From elementary all the way to high school, my most favorite subjects has always been in the area of art. Any class that had anything to do with drawing, coloring, or creating something out of nothing was going to be a class I knew I was going get a good grade in. This passion for art has reach a level I can't even fathom to measure. My bedroom walls was always covered with posters of cars and articles of all kinds of things that I've created and collected over the years growing up.

Now that I am a lot older, it's no longer my bedroom's wall that bares these art. Instead, it's my home's garage that are now filled with the actual things of the childhood's interest. Not all of it, but at least a few of them made into reality. I have accumulated ownership of over a dozen of vehicles over my adult years. From motorcycles to electric-hybrids Honda Insights to turbocharged Toyota MR2s; I did not have any discrimination towards any of these man made machine whatsoever. As long as it had some kind of appeal and affordability to me I knew I had to get my hands on it.

As time passes by, my taste for these machines became more rare and exotic. The appreciation for these types of art has always been on the broad side for me, but there is one thing on my mind that I would love to own in this lifetime...and that is an exotic high-performance car. Although I have not yet been in a car with more than 400 horse power and cost more than $100K, my senses of owning one is getting stronger and becoming more real; I can feel the accelerations pushing me back against my seat just from thinking about it. Amongst the many beautiful exotic high-performance cars available out there, the 2014 Porsche 991 GT3 is one that I would love to get my hands on the most. A Nissan GT-R is nice too, even a Ferrari 458 Italia looks amazing but there is something about the new GT3 that gets my heart beating fast every time I watch a clip of it on Youtube. Either ways, owning any one of these cars featuring in this coloring book would be considered a great achievement I would be grateful to accomplish in this lifetime.

For this particular book I've decided to focus on high-performance cars; cars that are rarely seen on the road. My passion for cars and art have led me to acquire the ability to render images into what you see now in this book. The process of rendering was very much a delicate task. In most areas of the images I had to precisely draw in the lines using the pen tool in Photoshop CS5; in particular was the contours, edges, and body panel gaps of the vehicles. In some of the images where there are clouds in the atmosphere were actually once an empty space of sky that had very little to nothing going on there. My goal for this book was to have it express as much details as possible. In doing so, I was able to produce the realistic looks that I believe is captivating to the eyes. Even though creating a coloring book the traditional way is the norm, I wanted to create one that is different from all the rest; one that is full of depths, shadows, highlights, and not of thick solid lines. I believe that this type of coloring book is going to be an evolution of fun coloring and sharing for everyone out there who enjoys applying colors onto paper.

Thank you for your interest in this coloring book. I am delighted to be able to share this creation with the world. I hope to inspire others as others have inspired me. Please share with me and others your finish work via **Instagram @Real_Coloring_Book and Facebook / Real Coloring Book.** I can't wait to see all of the finish work out there. Peace out!

TIP: Preserve this coloring book...copy image onto new paper. (For Personal use only)

2012 Ferrari 458 Italia

PERFORMANCE DATA: Vehicle Layout Mid-engine RWD 2-pass 2-door. Engine 4.5L V8 570-hp 398-lb-ft. Transmission 7-Speed Automatic w/Manual. Curb Weight 3042 lbs. Wheelbase 104.3 in. Length x Width x Height 178.2 x 76.3 x 47.8 in. 0-62 3.3 sec. Top Speed 202 mph. Base Price $237,259.

2012 Porsche 911 Turbo S

PERFORMANCE DATA: Vehicle Layout Rear-engine RWD 4-pass 2-door. Engine 3.8L Flat-6 Twin-Turbo 530-hp 516-lb-ft. Transmission 7-speed Automatic w/manual. Curb Weight 3550 lbs. Wheelbase 92.5 in. Length x Width x Height 175.2 x 72.9 x 51.2 in. 0-60 2.9 sec. Top Speed 195 mph. Base Price $160,000.

2012 Lamborghini Aventador LP700-4

PERFORMANCE DATA: Vehicle Layout Mid-engine AWD 2-pass 2-door. Engine 6.5L V12 691-hp 509-lb-ft. Transmission 7-speed Automatic w/Manual. Curb Weight 4085 lbs. Wheelbase 106.3 in. Length x Width x Height 188.2 x 79.9 x 44.7 in. 0-60 2.9 sec. Top Speed 217 mph. Base Price $379,700.

2013 Porsche 911 Carrera S

PERFORMANCE DATA: Vehicle Layout Rear-engine RWD 2-pass 2-door. Engine 3.8L Flat-6 400-hp 325-lb-ft. Transmission 7-Speed PDK Auto. Curb Weight 3075 lbs. Wheelbase 96.5 in. Length x Width x Height 176.8 x 71.2 x 51 in. 0-60 3.6 sec. Top Speed 190 mph. Base Price $108,000.

2014 Mercedes-Benz S63 AMG 4MATIC

PERFORMANCE DATA: Vehicle Layout Front-engine RWD 5-pass 4-door. Engine 5.5L V8 Bi-turbo 577-hp 664-lb-ft. Transmission 7-speed Automatic. Curb Weight 4806 lbs. Wheelbase 124.6 in. Length x Width x Height 206.5 x 74.8 x 58.8 in. 0-60 3.8 sec. Top Speed 187 mph. Base Price $142,375.

2012 Ferrari California Roadster

PERFORMANCE DATA: Vehicle Layout Front-engine RWD 2+2-pass 2-door Roadster. Engine 4.3L V8 483-hp 372-lb-ft. Transmission 7-speed Automated Manual. Curb Weight 3825 lbs. Wheelbase 105.1 in. Length x Width x Height 179.6 x 74.9 x 51.5 in. 0-60 3.9 sec. Top Speed 193 mph. Base Price $201,940.

2013 Mercedes-Benz CLS63 AMG

PERFORMANCE DATA: Vehicle Layout Front-engine, RWD, 4-pass, 4-door Engine 5.5L Twin-turbo V8 518-hp 516-lb-ft. Transmission 7-speed Automatic. Curb Weight 4275 lbs. Wheelbase 113.1 in. Length x Width x Height 196.7 x 74 x 55.3 in. 0-62 3.6 sec. Top Speed 186 mph. Base Price $96,805.

2008 Ferrari F430

PERFORMANCE DATA: Vehicle Layout Mid-engine RWD 2-pass 2-door. Engine 4.3L V8 490-hp 342-lb-ft. Transmission 6-speed Manual w/OD. Curb Weight 3197 lbs. Wheelbase 102.4 in. Length x Width x Height 177.6 x 75.7 x 47.8 in. 0-60 3.6 sec. Top Speed 186 mph. Base Price $190,000.

2005 Ford GT

PERFORMANCE DATA: Vehicle Layout Mid-engine RWD 2-pass 2-door. Engine 5.4L Supercharged V8 550-hp 500-lb-ft. Transmission 6-speed Manual. Curb Weight 3390 lbs. Wheelbase 106.7 in. Length x Width x Height 182.8 x 76.9 x 44.3 in. 0-60 3.3 sec. Top Speed 205 mph. Base Price $150,000.

2011 Lamborghini Gallardo LP560-4

PERFORMANCE DATA: Vehicle Layout Mid-engine 4WD 2-pass 2-door. Engine 5.2L V10 542-hp 398-lb-ft. Transmission 6-speed Manual. Curb Weight 3307 lbs. Wheelbase 100.8 in. Length x Width x Height 171.1 x 74.8 x 45.9 in. 0-60 3.8 sec. Top Speed 199 mph. Base Price $202,000.

2012 Maserati GranTurismo S

PERFORMANCE DATA: Vehicle Layout Front-engine RWD 4-pass 2-door. Engine 4.7L V8 454-hp 360-lb-ft. Transmission 6-speed Semi-Automatic. Curb Weight 4150 lbs. Wheelbase 115.8 in. Length x Width x Height 192.2 x 75.4 x 53.3 in. 0-60 4.8 sec. Top Speed 183 mph. Base Price $128,000.

2011 Porsche 911 GT2 RS

PERFORMANCE DATA: Vehicle Layout Rear-engine RWD 2-pass 2-door. Engine 3.6L Twin-turbo Flat-6 620-hp 516-lb-ft. Transmission 6-speed manual. Curb Weight 3075 lbs. Wheelbase 92.5 in. Length x Width x Height 175.9 x 72.9 x 50.6 in. 0-60 3.4 sec. Top Speed 205 mph. Base Price $245,950.

2012 Nissan GT-R

PERFORMANCE DATA: Vehicle Layout Front-engine AWD 4-pass 2-door. Engine 3.8L Twin-turbo V6 530-hp 448-lb-ft. Transmission 6-speed Automatic. Curb Weight 3859 lbs. Wheelbase 109.4 in. Length x Width x Height 183.1 x 74.9 x 54.0 in. 0-60 2.9 sec. Top Speed 191 mph. Base Price $90,000.

2012 BMW M3

PERFORMANCE DATA: Vehicle Layout Front-engine RWD 4-pass 2-door. Engine 4.0L V8 414-hp 295-lb-ft. Transmission 6-speed Manual. Curb Weight 3552 lbs. Wheelbase 108.7 in. Length x Width x Height 181.8 x 71.0 x 55.4 in. 0-60 4.3 sec. Top Speed n/a Base Price $66,125.

2013 BMW M5

PERFORMANCE DATA: Vehicle Layout Front-engine RWD 5-pass 4-door. Engine 4.4L V8 Twin-turbo 560-hp 500-lb-ft. Transmission 7-speed Automatic. Curb Weight 4387 lbs. Wheelbase 116.7 in. Length x Width x Height 193.5 x 74.4 x 57.3 in. 0-60 3.7 sec. Top Speed 190 mph Base Price $92,640.

2013 BMW M6

PERFORMANCE DATA: Vehicle Layout Front-engine RWD 4-pass 2-door. Engine 4.4L Twin-turbo V8 560-hp 500-lb-ft. Transmission 7-speed Automatic w/manual. Curb Weight 4250 lbs. Wheelbase 112.2 in. Length x Width x Height 193 x 74.8 x 54.1 in. 0-60 4.2 sec. Top Speed 155 mph. Base Price $112,850.

2013 Tesla Model S

PEFORMANCE DATA: Vehicle Layout Rear-motor RWD 7-pass 5-door Hatchback. Engine AC Permanent Magnet Synchronous Electric Motor 416-hp 443-lb-ft. Transmission 1-speed Direct Drive. Curb Weight 4650 lbs. Wheelbase 116.5 in. Length x Width x Height 196.0 x 77.3 x 56.5 in. 0-60 4.4 sec. Top Speed 133 mph. Base Price $58,570.

2012 McLaren MP4-12C Spyder

PERFORMANCE DATA: Vehicle Layout Mid-engine RWD 2-pass 2-door Conv. Engine 3.8L Twin-turbo V8 592-hp 443-lb-ft. Transmission 7-speed Automated Manual. Curb Weight 3161 lbs. Wheelbase 108 in. Length x Width x Height 177.4 x 75.2 x 47.2 in. 0-60 3.0 sec. Top Speed 205 mph. Base Price $230,000.

2010 Lamborghini Murcielago LP640

PERFORMANCE DATA: Vehicle Layout Mid-engine RWD 2-pass 2-door. Engine 6.5L V12 632-hp 487-lb-ft. Transmission 6-speed manual w/OD. Curb Weight 3671 lbs. Wheelbase 104.9 in. Length x Width x Height 181.5 x 81.0 x 44.7 in. 0-60 3.4 sec. Top Speed 211 mph. Base Price $354,000.

2013 Porsche Panamera GTS

PERFORMANCE DATA: Vehicle Layout Front-engine AWD 4-pass 5-door Hatchback. Engine 430-hp 348-lb-ft. Transmission 7-speed Twin-Clutch Auto. Curb Weight 4367 lbs. Wheelbase 115.0 in. Length x Width x Height 195.7 x 76.0 x 55.4 in. 0-60 4.1 sec. Top Speed 175 mph. Base Price $111,975.

2012 Audi R8

PERFORMANCE DATA: Vehicle Layout Mid-engine RWD 2-pass 2-door. Engine 5.2L V10 525-hp 391-lb-ft. Transmission 7-speed S Tronic. Curb Weight 3605 lbs. Wheelbase 104.3 in. Length x Width x Height 174.6 x 76.0 x 49.3 in. 0-60 3.7 sec. Top Speed 196 mph. Base Price $155,000.

2009 Ferrari 430 Scuderia

PERFORMANCE DATA: Vehicle Layout Mid-engine RWD 2-pass 2-door coupe. Engine 4.3L V8 510-hp 347-lb-ft. Transmission 6-speed Semi-Automatic F1 gearbox. Curb Weight 2975 lb. Wheelbase 102.4 in. Length x Width x Height 177.6 x 75.7 x 47.2 in. 0-60 3.5 sec. Top Speed 198 mph. Base Price $313,300.

2010 Mercedes-Benz SL65 AMG

PERFORMNACE DATA: Vehicle Layout Front-engine RWD 2-pass 2-door Conv. Engine 6.0L Twin-turbo V12 621-hp 738-lb-ft. Transmission 5-speed Auto. Curb Weight 4274 lbs. Wheelbase 108 in. Length x Width x Height 178.5 x 71.5 x 51 in. 0-60 3.6 sec. Top Speed 199 mph. Base Price $300,000.

2006 Mercedes-Benz SLR McLaren

PERFORMANCE DATA: Vehicle Layout Front-engine RWD 2-pass 2-door. Engine 5.4L Supercharged V8 617-hp 575-lb-ft. Transmission 5-Speed Automatic. Curb Weight 3748 lbs. Wheelbase 110 in. Length x Width x Height 193.3 x 75.1 x 49.6 in. 0-60 3.8 sec. Top Speed 208 mph. Base Price $450,000.

2013 Mercedes-Benz SLS AMG GT

PERFORMANCE DATA: Vehicle Layout Front-engine RWD 2-pass 2-door. Engine 6.2L V8 583-hp 479-lb-ft. Transmission 7-speed Automatic w/manual. Curb Weight 3761 lbs. Wheelbase 105.5 in. Length x Width x Height 182.6 x 76.3 x 49.7 in. 0-60 3.8 sec. Top Speed 197 mph. Base Price $202,000.

2013 Chevrolet Corvette Z06

PERFORMANCE DATA: Vehicle Layout Front-engine RWD 2-pass 2-door. Engine 7.0L V8 505-hp 470-lb-ft. Transmission 6-Speed Manual. Curb Weight 3175 lbs. Wheelbase 105.7 in. Length x Width x Height 175.6 x 75.9 x 48.7 in. 0-60 3.5 sec. Top Speed 198 mph. Base Price $76,592.

2006 Bugatti 16.4 Veyron

PERFORMANCE DATA: Vehicle Layout Mid-engine 4WD 2-pass 2-door. Engine 8.0L W16 4-turbo 1001-hp 923-lb-ft. Transmission 7-speed DSG Automatic. Curb Weight 4162 lbs. Wheelbase 106.7 in. Length x Width x Height 175.7 x 78.7 x 47.4 in. 0-60 2.6 sec. Top Speed 253 mph. Base Price $1,440,000.

2013 Dodge Viper SRT

PERFORMANCE DATA: Vehicle Layout Front-engine RWD 2-pass 2-door. Engine 8.4L V10 640 hp 600 lb-ft. Transmission 6-speed Manual. Curb Weight 3300 lbs. Wheelbase 98.7 in. Length x Width x Height 175.1 x 76.4 x 49.1 in 0-60 3.7 sec. Top Speed 206 mph. Base Price $138,340.

Reference

For performance data and base price references - go to the websites below and enter in year, make, and model of vehicles.

Caranddriver.com
Edmunds.com
Wikipedia.com
Topspeed.com
Roadandtrack.com
Motortrend.com
Conceptcarz.com

Disclaimer: All information provided in this book regarding the vehicles performance data and base price may not be fully accurate per manufacture's specification.

Made in the USA
San Bernardino, CA
15 January 2015